AXIS

A PARENT'S GUIDE TO

LGBTQ+ &
YOUR TEEN

axis

Tyndale House Publishers
Carol Stream, Illinois

Visit Tyndale online at tyndale.com.

Visit Axis online at axis.org.

Tyndale and Tyndale's quill logo are registered trademarks of Tyndale House Ministries.

A Parent's Guide to LGBTQ+ & Your Teen

Scripture quotations are taken from the Holy Bible, *New International Version,*® *NIV.*® Copyright © 1973, 1978, 1984, 2011 by Biblica, Inc.® Used by permission. All rights reserved worldwide.

For information about special discounts for bulk purchases, please contact Tyndale House Publishers at csresponse@tyndale.com, or call 1-855-277-9400.

Library of Congress Cataloging-in-Publication Data

A catalog record for this book is available from the Library of Congress.

ISBN 978-1-4964-6738-6

Printed in the United States of America

29	28	27	26	25	24	23
7	6	5	4	3	2	1

You don't have to label your sexuality; so many kids these days are not labeling their sexuality and I think that's so cool. . . . If you like something one day then you do, and if you like something else the other day, it's whatever. You don't have to label yourself because it's not set in stone. It's so fluid.

**LILY-ROSE DEPP,
JOHNNY DEPP'S DAUGHTER**

CONTENTS

A LETTER FROM AXIS

Dear Reader,

We're Axis, and since 2007, we've been creating resources to help connect parents, teens, and Jesus in a disconnected world. We're a group of gospel-minded researchers, speakers, and content creators, and we're excited to bring you the best of what we've learned about making meaningful connections with the teens in your life.

This parent's guide is designed to help start a conversation. Our goal is to give you enough knowledge that you're able to ask your teen informed questions about their world. For each guide, we spend weeks reading, researching, and interviewing parents and teens in order to distill everything you need to know about the topic at hand. We encourage you to read the whole thing and then to use the questions we include to get the conversation going with your teen—and then to follow the conversation wherever it leads.

As Douglas Stone, Bruce Patton, and Sheila Heen point out in their book *Difficult Conversations*, "Changes in attitudes and behavior rarely come about because of arguments, facts, and attempts to persuade. How often do *you* change your values and beliefs—or whom you love or what you want in life—based on something someone tells you? And how likely are you to do so when the person who is trying to change you doesn't seem fully aware of the reasons you see things differently in the first place?"[1] For whatever reason, when we believe that others are trying to understand *our* point of view, our defenses usually go down, and we're more willing to listen to *their* point of view. The rising generation is no exception.

So we encourage you to ask questions, to listen, and then to share your heart with your teen. As we often say at Axis, discipleship happens where conversation happens.

Sincerely,
Your friends at Axis

---

[1] Douglas Stone, Bruce Patton, and Sheila Heen, *Difficult Conversations: How to Discuss What Matters Most*, rev. ed. (New York: Penguin Books, 2010), 137.

TODAY'S TEENS RELY ON THE INTERNET, DISLIKE LABELS, AND LOVE THEIR LGBTQ+ FRIENDS

IN THE 1990S, BEING GAY was more controversial than it is now. Ellen DeGeneres sparked controversy in 1997 for coming out as a lesbian on her hit TV show. In recent years, Ellen's daytime talk show became one of the most popular,[1] and at the end of 2016, President Obama awarded her the Presidential Medal of Freedom.[2]

Modern teens are growing up in a culture that has changed significantly since the '90s. If they aren't questioning their own sexuality, they have friends who are. They're living in a society where Harry Styles is modeling Gucci's womenswear[3] and where there are so many letters in the current LGBTQ+ initialism (LGBTQQIAAP)[4] that it's simpler to use a plus sign than to list all of them. It's no longer as big a deal to explore what it means to be gay or bisexual. Young people now tend to focus more on the newer terms represented by the acronym: *queer*, *questioning*, *intersex*, *ally*, *asexual*, and *pansexual*.

Even if your kids don't struggle with their sexual orientation or gender identity, they probably know people who do. For the most part, the way the church has addressed these issues has been inadequate at best and polarizing at worst. What follows is what we think you need to know about what is shaping Gen Z's perceptions of these issues, as well as how you can engage well with your teen and the LGBTQ+ community.

WHAT TERMS DO I NEED TO KNOW?

BEFORE WE GET INTO the theological or moral concepts surrounding this issue, let's define our terms. You've probably heard of many of these labels but may not have had great working definitions up until now.

Something to keep in mind as you read through these terms is that Gen Z tends to view gender as something of a spectrum, as opposed to the traditional binary view of sexuality as either masculine or feminine. They commonly view gender and sexuality as disconnected from each other (although younger people who disagree with this viewpoint do exist[5]). YouTuber Brendan Jordan explains it like this: "Sexuality is who you go to bed with, and gender identity is who you go to bed *as*."[6] Understanding sexuality to be so broad in scope means there are many ways to define it. *Having the right label is not nearly as important to many younger people as not needing to have any label at all,* as per our opening quote. Each individual is the highest authority when it comes to defining his or her sexuality.

(For the following list, we've relied on the websites It's Pronounced Metrosexual[7] and We Are Family.[8])

Ally: Anyone who supports the LGBTQ+ community

Androgynous: Having both male and female characteristics or not having characteristics that clearly distinguish one as male or female

Asexual: Experiencing no or little sexual interest in anyone

Bisexual: Sexually attracted to both men and women

Cisgender: Someone whose gender identity matches his or her biological sex; anyone who is not transgender

Closeted: Someone who conceals his or her LGBTQ+ gender or sexual identity

Coming out: The process of revealing one's LGBTQ+ gender or sexual identity

Cross-dresser: Someone who wears the clothing of a different gender or sex; does not necessarily reflect the person's actual gender identity or sexual orientation

Demisexual: Someone who does not experience sexual attraction until forming an emotional attachment

Drag king: A woman who dresses as a man, exaggerating masculine characteristics in a theatrical way

Drag queen: A man who dresses as a woman, exaggerating feminine characteristics in a theatrical way

Gay: Someone attracted to members of the same sex/gender; can refer to either men or women

Gender and sexual diversity (GSD): A term that some people prefer to any of the LGBTQ+ initialisms because of the lack of a need to specify each of the identities it covers.

Gender expression: How each person manifests gender; could be tied to the individual's gender identity or could be a social construct

Gender fluid: Not identifying as any particular gender

Gender identity: How someone perceives his or her gender

Genderqueer: Catchall term for people who identify as various nontraditional gender identities; used for gender as opposed to sexual orientation

Heteronormative: The idea that there are only two genders/ sexualities, i.e., male and female, and that everyone falls into either of those categories; considered oppressive and restricting

Heterosexual ("straight"): Someone whose gender and biological sex align and who is attracted to members of the opposite sex

Hermaphrodite: Outmoded, stigmatizing term referring to someone who has both male and female genitalia or other sexual characteristics outside of the biological norms for male and female; preferred term is *intersex* (see below)

Homophobia: Any negative posture toward LGBTQ+ people

Homosexual: Outdated term for describing people who are attracted to members of the same gender or sex; preferred term is *gay* (see above)

Intersex: Someone with sexual organs, chromosomes, hormones, etc., that diverge from the typical male and female biological pattern; the term that has replaced *hermaphrodite*

Lesbian: A woman who is sexually attracted to other women

Nonbinary: Identifying as something other than the traditional binary genders of male and female

Something to keep in mind as you read through these terms is that Gen Z tends to view gender as something of a spectrum, as opposed to the traditional binary view of sexuality as either masculine or feminine.

Metrosexual: A man who spends more care on his appearance than is traditionally considered normal for men

Out: As a verb, meaning to forcibly expose someone else's LGBTQ+ gender or sexual orientation; as an adjective, describing someone who is public about his or her LGBTQ+ gender or sexual orientation

Pansexual ("pan"): Someone who is attracted to people of any kind of gender or sexual identity

Polyamory ("poly"): Having multiple romantic and/or sexual partners at one time

Queer: Way of referring to the entire LGBTQ+ community; can be considered offensive if used by people outside the community

Questioning: Someone who is exploring his or her gender or sexual identity

Transgender ("trans"): Someone who identifies with a gender other than the one that corresponds to his or her biological sex

Transsexual: Someone who identifies with a gender different from his or her biological sex and who undergoes surgery so that the two will correspond (sometimes considered an outdated and offensive term)

Transvestite: Someone who dresses in clothing associated with the opposite sex (does not necessarily mean that the person is transgender or any particular gender or sexual orientation)

Zie/hir: One set of many proposed gender-neutral pronouns; some also use the plural pronoun *they* in place of *he* or *she*

When referring to people in the LGBTQ+ community, we should avoid certain phraseology. Stay away from the phrase "the gay lifestyle." Don't call someone "a transgender" or "transgendered." These terms imply that the people in question are set apart in a negative way, and it also implies there is only one "lifestyle" or way of being gay. Nobody refers to "the heterosexual lifestyle" when discussing opposite-sex-attracted individuals.

In addition, those in the LGBTQ+ community will likely be offended by anything implying that sexual orientation is a choice (i.e., "sexual preference") or associating them with pedophilia or other deviant practices. It should go without saying that we should avoid any language that is derogatory, including terms such as *fag*, *dyke*, *tranny*, or *she-man*. For other terminology that the LGBTQ+ community considers offensive, see the We Are Family link referenced above (https://wearefamilycharleston.org/lgbt-glossary-az), as well as the glossary of terms from GLAAD (https://www.glaad.org/reference/terms).[9] *Using the appropriate language with individuals in the LGBTQ+ community can build trust and potentially lead to a transformational relationship.* Don't worry about the notion that using the correct terminology is affirming someone's sexual decisions; simply reach out and meet them where they are. By caring about them as they are, you will earn the right to be heard if and when the opportunity arises.

Don't worry about the notion that using the correct terminology is affirming someone's sexual decisions; simply reach out and meet them where they are. By caring about them as they are, you will earn the right to be heard if and when the opportunity arises.

HOW DOES GEN Z VIEW LGBTQ+ ISSUES?

GEN Z IS LOOSELY DEFINED as those who were born between 1999 and 2015. Those on the older end of this spectrum generally think LGBTQ+ issues are important. They are empathetic toward those in the LGBTQ+ community. Barna has found that members of Gen Z are twice as likely as millennials to be atheists or to identify as part of the LGBTQ+ community. Around 69 percent see no problem with someone identifying as transgender, and about a third of them know someone who is transgender.[10] *Independent* reports that only about two-thirds of Gen Z say they are completely heterosexual: "This is in stark contrast to older generations, with 88 percent of baby boomers (aged 52 to 71) and 85 percent of Generation X (aged 38 to 51) identifying as purely heterosexual."[11] This is not to say that LGBTQ+ issues are not still controversial. But as far as *the cultural discussion* goes, people have generally accepted that identifying as LGBTQ+ is normal.

TODAY'S TEENS TEND TO MAKE JUDGMENTS based *not* on what the Bible or their parents say, but on their own feelings, their empathy for others, what their friends think, the internet, and pop culture.

PEOPLE THEY KNOW AND LOVE

It's one thing to talk about LGBTQ+ concerns as an abstract concept; it's another altogether if your best friend or one of your family members is wrestling with gender confusion and/or sexual preference. One study from GLSEN (Gay, Lesbian & Straight Education Network) found that "students who knew someone who was LGBT held less negative attitudes towards LGBT people than students who did not know any LGBT people."[12]

Dr. Juli Slattery of Authentic Intimacy describes meeting a mother whose young daughter experiences gender dysphoria.[13]

WHAT IS SHAPING GEN Z'S PERSPECTIVE ON LGBTQ+ ISSUES?

The pain of that struggle is daily and acute. The daughter will break down sobbing because she hates the clothes she has to wear. Something as simple as taking a shower is a traumatic experience. Imagine if your son or daughter had a close friend in this situation. Perhaps they do. Many teens rely on their feelings as indicators of truth, so when they observe someone they care about strongly feeling a certain way, they tend to accept that those feelings indicate truth about reality. There's a positive side to this, though—empathy also humanizes the issue. Older generations often tend to forget that these are real people struggling with or trying to make sense of their sexual urges and sexual identity.

MOVIES, TV SHOWS, AND MUSIC

Media is a powerful influencer of how people see the world. Quite a few celebrities identify as part of the LGBTQ+ community,[14] and more LGBTQ+ characters appear in movies and TV shows now than in previous decades. A few movies that received a lot of attention at the Oscars recently were *Moonlight* (2016) and *Call Me by Your Name* (2017). *Moonlight* was extremely compelling because, rather than being an argument, it portrayed a gay man's struggles in a moving and sympathetic way. *Love, Simon* (2018) is a romantic dramedy about a closeted gay teen coming to terms with his identity. *Every Day* (2018) tells the story of a girl who falls in love with a person who wakes up in a different male or female body every day, normalizing the idea that gender and sexuality are irrelevant if you really love someone. Netflix's *Everything Sucks!* (canceled after only one season) was an ode to the '90s whose main storyline focused on a girl discovering that she is same-sex attracted. Most recently, Disney made public their goal of "advancing representation in front of and behind the camera," specifically highlighting LGBTQ+ people and ethnic minorities as "underrepresented groups."[15]

Plenty of pop icons vocally support the LGBTQ+ community and/or identify as part of it. Lil Nas X did so provocatively with his music video for "MONTERO (Call Me by Your Name)," and accompanying promotional stunts. He said, "I 100% want to represent the LGBT community."[16] Lady Gaga has been another notable example.[17] Miley Cyrus is outspoken on LGBTQ+ issues and identifies as pansexual.[18] Halsey identifies as bisexual.[19] Rita Ora collaborated with other megastars Charli XCX, Bebe Rexha, and Cardi B to create "Girls," a song about sometimes wanting to kiss girls. Though the song has faced

Today's teens tend to make judgments based not on what the Bible or their parents say, but on their own feelings, their empathy for others, what their friends think, the internet, and pop culture.

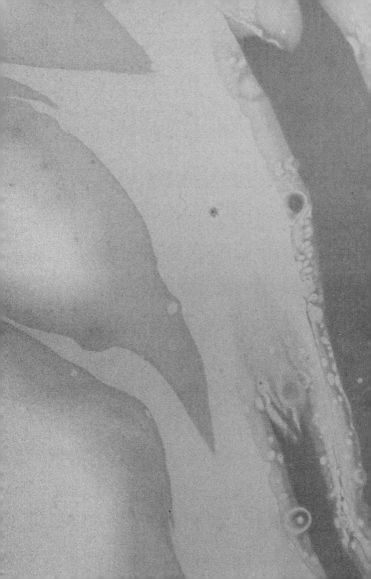

some backlash, both Ora and Cardi B have responded by saying that it reflects their experiences with other women.

Pop star Hayley Kiyoko is not only openly gay but also has many songs about same-sex attraction, notably "Girls Like Girls."[20] When discussing the importance of LGBTQ+ icons in media, Kiyoko told *Billboard*, "If you see two girls falling in love and normalizing that, then [people] can go, 'I can fall in love, too.' . . . If they see that, then they can believe it. It's just how we are."[21]

Taylor Swift, who is well known for writing many songs about her relationships with men, defended Kiyoko when the latter was criticized for singing so often about her attraction to women.[22] Swift also released a music video in 2019 expressing her support for the LGBTQ+ community.[23]

Johnny Depp's daughter, Lily-Rose Depp, participated in the Self Evident Truths project, the brainchild of photographer iO Tillet Wright, whose goal was to photograph 10,000 people who identify as anything other than straight.[24] The project's purpose was to humanize the LGBTQ+ community and to combat discrimination. Many people thought Depp's support of the campaign was her way of coming out as gay, but she says that was not her intention. What she actually wanted to do was communicate that she doesn't identify as 100 percent straight, and she wants people to know they don't have to label their sexuality.[25]

THE INTERNET

It's difficult to overestimate the influence the internet has over teens' perceptions of LGBTQ+ issues. One mom told us that the internet is her biggest competition as a parent. If she disagrees with her children on anything, all they have to do is go online, where they can quickly find many people who will validate their beliefs.

We know a Christian dad who has one child who identifies as a lesbian and one who identifies as transgender. He says, "The web shapes kids' perceptions of sexuality and gender," and that Tumblr has been particularly significant in validating his kids' current sexual and gender identities. The internet can also introduce these concepts or labels in developmentally inappropriate ways, meaning that preadolescent kids who may not even know what sex is have already been introduced to the normalization of same-sex attraction. Before they've experienced any sexual urges, they're taught that all their urges are valid and should be explored. The internet offers easy access to communities that are accepting and supportive, something the church often is not. These communities are available across the platforms of the web (one example being Amino).

The dad notes that kids tend to treat the internet in the same way that some people use WebMD. It's easy to go to WebMD, search your symptoms, and let the website "diagnose" you (whether accurately or inaccurately). Sure, it's somewhat helpful to go online with medical questions, but it doesn't compare to actually meeting with your doctor. Kids often use the internet in the same way when it comes to their gender confusion. They search online for information about their experiences and rely on the results to explain what those experiences mean, rather than talking to parents, teachers, or pastors.

YOUTUBE

YouTube is another important platform when it comes to shaping the perceptions of young people. The site has made it possible for us to get a glimpse into the lives of everyday people around the world. As a result, people who are wrestling with their gender identities can share their thoughts and beliefs with whoever is willing to listen. So your teens could watch Connor Franta's coming-out video, which currently has over 12 million views.[26] Or they could watch Milo Stewart's videos exploring his sexual identity.[27] Or they could watch Nikkie de Jager from NikkiTutorials emotionally share about being transgender (currently with over 38 million views).[28] These videos show average people, just like our teens and their friends, grappling with their sexual confusion and taking stands on what they believe.

One mom told us that the internet is her biggest competition as a parent. If she disagrees with her children on anything, all they have to do is go online, where they can quickly find many people who will validate their beliefs.

ARE THERE OTHER WAYS GENDER CONFUSION IS IMPACTING OUR LIVES?

THERE ARE MYRIAD OTHER WAYS gender confusion is shaping and will continue to shape modern life. Several years ago, Facebook gave users the option to choose among 50 different genders.[29] We spoke with a guy who is in his twenties and working at a university in California. At the beginning of his daily meetings, he and his colleagues are required to go around the room and say which pronouns they want people to apply to them that day. We also spoke to a woman in her thirties who, when auditioning for a play in Colorado Springs, was asked to put her preferred pronoun on the contact information sheet. Some gender-fluid people are even using colored bracelets so their friends know which pronouns to use for them each day.

WHAT ARE THE CULTURAL VALUES THAT HAVE LED US HERE?

IF YOU GO ONLINE AND READ the positions of people who identify in ways that would have been shocking to most of society only a few decades ago, you'll notice that their beliefs are simply a logical out-working of cultural values we've held for a while now. One is that an individual's happiness is the highest good: whatever makes you happy is what you should pursue. Another is that our feelings dictate the truth. (Think about how many Disney movies encourage viewers to follow their hearts, i.e., their feelings.) If we feel a particular way, those feelings determine our identities and our destinies. Singer and actress Keke Palmer says:

> I don't belong to anyone else but myself. I have to make my own decisions. Happiness is defined by me. My sexuality is defined by me . . . and I can make it what I want

to make it because I'm the one who makes that choice.[30]

Our culture also idolizes romance and sexuality: romantic relationships are viewed as the best kind of relationships, surpassing friendship or camaraderie. In addition, secular culture sees the idea of not being sexually active as bizarre, laughable, and unhealthy. In order to be fully human, one must be sexually active. Many pop songs about heterosexual love portray romance as the ultimate good and happiness—a dangerous idea because it means that losing this love is devastating. The song "SAD!" by XXXTentacion [*warning: strong language*] is one example of what happens when we look to romantic love as the ultimate happiness and then lose it.[31] American movies almost always have a romantic plotline, as though stories that focus on families or friendship will not be able to keep our attention. (The church itself often emphasizes marriage so much that singles ministries may exist mainly to make it easier to find a spouse, communicating that singleness is a lesser, unfulfilling lifestyle.)

So what does this have to do with the LGBTQ+ community? Well, for example, if romantic love is the best kind of love there is, then saying that same-sex marriage is wrong is denying same-sex-attracted people the best kind of love there is. By idolizing marriage and by not upholding singleness as a valuable, holy, and *desirable* calling, we communicate that people who identify as LGBTQ+ must live less fulfilling lives than the ones straight people get to enjoy. And if sexual satisfaction or gratification is not only a right but a virtue, how can anyone deny LGBTQ+ individuals their license for pleasure?

If you go online and read the positions of people who identify in ways that would have been shocking to most of society only a few decades ago, you'll notice that their beliefs are simply a logical outworking of cultural values we've held for a while now.

HOW HAS THE CHURCH RESPONDED POORLY TO THE LGBTQ+ COMMUNITY?

IN EPISODE TWO of the *Q Ideas* podcast,[32] author and speaker Dr. Preston Sprinkle says that the majority of LGBTQ+ people who have left the church have done so not over theological differences, but because of the condemnation and dehumanization they experienced there. Some of the church's failings in this area include:

- Treating homosexuality as a sin that is worse and more repulsive than other sins

- Not challenging heterosexual sins—such as porn use, adultery, or premarital sex—as frequently as homosexual sins

- Speaking about the LGBTQ+ community in a way that is derogatory or portrays them as our enemies

- Not valuing the single life

- Ignoring the LGBTQ+ community or those struggling with same-sex attraction

- Oversimplifying the LGBTQ+ experience

The church has also arguably failed to speak compellingly about what it means to be a man or a woman. In the BBC's video "Things Not to Say to a Non-Binary Person" several nonbinary people discuss questions that they consider ignorant and offensive. In the middle of the video, almost as a throwaway, one of them asks, "What is a man, and what is a woman?"[33] Those are important and foundational questions. If we cannot answer them clearly, it's no wonder culture rejects our position.

In contrast to condemnation or apathy in the church is the "affirming response." This is the position held by Matthew Vines or Jen Hatmaker—that God approves of and endorses active LGBTQ+ sexual expressions.[34] While this position is taking significant liberties with the biblical narrative and seeks to ignore or discount specific scriptural instruction, those who hold it often do so out of deep empathy for those in the LGBTQ+ community. This empathy is something we can learn from, even if we disagree with their conclusion.

HOW CAN THE CHURCH RESPOND WELL?

WE BELIEVE THAT THE BEST response the church can have is to be an incarnational witness to the love, truth, respect, and dignity that Jesus afforded to every human being. In so doing, we model Christ's unconditional love and desire for everyone to live lives of holiness. Jesus met people where they were and called them to a deeper understanding of truth, goodness, and righteousness. He built relationships with those whom the religious leaders rejected. Scripture reminds us that Jesus ate with sinners and tax collectors, that women of ill repute followed Him, and that He refused to despise or reject anyone who humbly called on His name.

WHAT THE BIBLE SAYS

The Bible clearly defines what both ancient Israel and the early church believed about godly sexuality. The only kind of romantic relationship either ever endorses outright is that between one man and one woman, beginning with God's institution of marriage in Genesis 1 and 2. It's true that ancient Israel practiced polygamy for a time in the Old Testament, but it's evident that this position was never part of God's plan, and both the Old Testament and New Testament never portray polygamy as something positive.[35]

When asked a question about marriage in Matthew 19, Jesus refers to Genesis 1 and 2 as a basis for His answer.[36] Paul gives us an even deeper understanding of marriage in Ephesians 5:32, when he reveals "a profound mystery," i.e., that marriage is a unique picture of Christ's relationship with the church. Christ is the masculine archetype and the church is the feminine archetype that individual men and women model in imperfect ways. These

We believe that the best response the church can have is to be an incarnational witness to the love, truth, respect, and dignity that Jesus afforded to every human being.

archetypes will not disappear in the new heavens and the new earth but rather will culminate in the marriage supper of the Lamb, when Christ finally weds the bride he died to redeem. Our sexuality matters because God is its Creator (and so has the right to define it). But it also matters because, as Dr. Slattery says, our "sexuality is a holy metaphor of a God who invites us into covenant with Himself."[37] It follows that if we abuse our sexuality, we are living out a lie about God's love, who He is, and how we relate to Him.

HOW TO COMMUNICATE THOSE TRUTHS

Jesus was aggressive with the hypocritical religious leaders of His day, but He was gentle with the sinners and outcasts—those whom society viewed as repulsive. He spent time with them. He ate food with them. He is the model we should look to when determining how to

interact with those with whom we disagree. We should not worry that spending time with such people will "tarnish
our witness." Dr. Sprinkle notes that Jesus
didn't stop loving people simply because
spending time with them gave Him a bad
reputation:

> If people mistake your unconditional
> love for gay people as an affirmation
> of homosexual behavior, then
> don't worry about it. You're in good
> company. Religious people often
> thought that Jesus was a sinner
> because he had many friends
> who were sinners, yet he kept on
> befriending sinners.[38]

Obviously, the fact that Jesus loved sinners does not mean that He compro-
mised His holiness. Jesus showed love
and respect to the woman at the well

Jesus didn't stop loving people simply because spending time with them gave Him a bad reputation.

in John 4 and was far more open with her about who He was than He was with the hypocritical Pharisees. But He also confronted her about her sin so that she could experience true life and flourishing. He is the example we should follow.

WHAT ARE SOME PRACTICAL THINGS I CAN DO?

1. LOVE YOUR NEIGHBOR AS YOURSELF.

The first and most important thing we must do is love people where and as they are. If your kids come out to you, your immediate reaction needs to be to hug them and make it absolutely clear that you still love them and that your love for them will never change. The dad we mentioned earlier said, "If you don't hug your kid right after they come out, you've blown it." This is the most important message he wishes he could get across to parents whose kids have not yet come out. Imagine what it would be like if you brought your fiancé home to your parents, and they reacted with disgust or hatred. That's what it will seem like if you react badly when your child comes out. If your kids have already come out, and you've already reacted badly, apologizing will go a long way. It will be harder to restore trust in that situation, but definitely apologize to your kids and do what you can to make up for the hurt you've caused them.

Make sure your kids know that your love for them will never waver, no matter what happens, and that you will never give up on your relationship with them. In the short film "Dear Church: I'm Gay," several people talk about their struggles with same-sex attraction and their journeys toward God.[39] Parents Brad and Robin Harper describe how their first response when their son Drew came out to them was to panic. But throughout the years that followed, they say that by far the most important step they took was never cutting off their relationship with him, no matter how he chose to live.

2. DON'T PANIC—PLAY THE LONG GAME.

We've already mentioned the *Q Ideas* podcast, and we specifically recommend episodes one to six as a resource on LGBTQ+ issues. In episode three, Dr. Russell Moore notes that when children fail in some way, there is a tendency for parents to feel that their kids' behavior is a judgment on their parenting. It's important that if you have a child who struggles with his or her gender identity or sexual orientation, you don't see that struggle as a judgment on how you've done as a parent. If you do, you will likely be tempted to "fix" your child as a way of validating yourself. And if your main goal is to fix them, they will become a project to master, not a child to love.

If your teen comes out to you, it's not the end of the world. Remember your own adolescence? That was a tumultuous time for most of us. Many people regard their teenage years as periods when they were figuring out who they were and made many mistakes along the way. Also, people change a lot as they grow up. Just because your kids identify one way today does not mean that they will continue to do so forever.

So don't jump to conclusions or try to fix them. Spend more time learning where they're coming from—their situation will give you a lot to talk about. The dad with the two LGBTQ+ kids said, "The scariest thing that can happen to me as a parent is if my kids disappear," that is, if he loses them to the internet or their friends. Even if he dislikes what his kids are saying, he's grateful that they at least still want to share their lives with him.

3. BE A GOOD LISTENER.
Loving people well means listening to them well. This principle applies any time we're talking to someone with

whom we strongly disagree. In the episode "Listening So People Will Talk" of the *Java with Juli* podcast, Becky Harling observes, "In order for people to feel loved, they have to feel heard."[40] Until people feel loved, heard, and respected, they will not listen or be open to what you have to say. This goes for *anyone* with any variety of belief. For example, Westboro Baptist Church is notorious for its hatred of the LGBTQ+ community, perpetuating every stereotype culture has of Christians being hateful and condemning. It would be incredibly easy in turn to hate the members of Westboro Baptist for their behavior. However, one girl who left the church did so because people outside the church were willing to love her as she was. Because they treated her with love and respect, she was open to hearing what they had to say and to changing her position.[41]

It's important that if
you have a child who
struggles with his or her
gender identity or sexual
orientation, you don't see
that struggle as a judgment
on how you've done as
a parent.

Too often we have an "us versus them" mentality. We are more worried about the "gay agenda" taking over our country than we are about the broken people next door to us. *It is* vital *to remember that everyone struggles with some form of temptation— ours just might be easier to hide.* Imagine your most secret sin being broadcast to your coworkers or friends. This is what many kids feel like when they finally gain the courage to share their temptations. We have *all* sinned and fallen short of God's glory, and the ground is level at the foot of the cross.[42] Remember, we are missionaries to the people in our spheres. Missionaries aren't shocked when unbelievers sin; instead, they do their best to share the love and truth of Christ with them.

4. EDUCATE YOURSELF ON LGBTQ+ ISSUES.

Our goal in listening should not be to win an argument or to change people. It should be to show people we love them, to learn about their experiences, and to empathize with them. It's not helpful if Christians go around telling people who have never been attracted to the opposite sex that their sexuality is a choice. It's not helpful if we have no understanding of the pain and suffering that people in the LGBTQ+ community often experience.

We do great damage through our ignorance. If we're willing to educate ourselves on these topics, we will speak with greater accuracy, credibility, and compassion. When you meet people who identify as LGBTQ+, expressing curiosity and interest in their lives shows that you care about them. Learn the terminology we mentioned earlier because it's the language your kids are using. Become familiar with the Human Rights Campaign (HRC), the largest LGBTQ+

community in the country. If you want to know what the LGBTQ+ community values, you need to follow the HRC—*especially* if your kids identify as LGBTQ+. See also the other resources throughout this guide, as well as the Additional Resources section at the end.

5. BE HOSPITABLE.

As we already noted, Jesus ate and drank with sinners. Christian speaker and teacher Kevin Bywater says, "Hospitality may be the greatest bulwark against both hostility and hypocrisy."[43] It's easy to "share God's truth" in a hypocritical way, condemning same-sex attraction while turning a blind eye to our own sins. But another danger is sharing the truth in a hostile way akin to the "clanging cymbal" Paul mentions in 1 Corinthians 13:1. Hospitality helps us avoid both errors. If we are hospitable, we give of

DISCUSSION QUESTIONS

- The church has responded poorly in many ways, especially by stigmatizing those in the LGBTQ+ community.

- We can learn from Gen Z's desire to love everyone (and remember that Jesus Himself associated with sinners all the time).

- We can do many things to build bridges with the LGBTQ+ community and help our kids have a biblical framework. The best possible thing we can do is remember that Christ Himself—not our sexuality—is where we find fulfillment.

We can do many things
to build bridges with the
LGBTQ+ community
and help our kids have a
biblical framework. The
best possible thing we can
do is remember that Christ
Himself—not our sexuality—
is where we find fulfillment.

- If the Gen Zers in your life aren't questioning their sexuality or gender, they definitely know at least one person who is.

- Using appropriate terminology will help us build relationships with and relate to those in the LGBTQ+ community.

- Today's teens tend to make judgments based not on what the Bible or their parents say, but on their own feelings, their empathy for others, what their friends think, the internet, and pop culture.

- Values such as happiness being the highest virtue, feelings dictating truth, and sex and romantic love being the ultimate pursuit have influenced our culture's view of LGBTQ+ issues.

RECAP

to be heterosexual or cisgender? Will that save them? No. In contrast to *anything* we cling to in this world, make our idols from, or find fulfillment in, *Jesus Himself is what we need—nothing more.* No matter what sexuality or gender we identify with, *our sexuality cannot fulfill us.* So rather than trying hard to convince others to have a certain view of sexuality and gender, we must point them to Christ above all. Knowing, loving, and following Him are central. If we can offer someone Christ, He'll deal with the rest according to His infinite wisdom and in His omniscient timing. He will convict and correct. That could take years or even decades. Are we ready to rest in the knowledge that He is firmly in control and at work, even when we don't see or understand it?

media that normalizes LGBTQ+ behaviors. If this is one of your goals, we would encourage you to try to be consistent by not watching media that normalizes *any* sinful sexual behaviors. Sex outside of marriage is so accepted in our culture now that many people don't think twice about watching TV shows that make it seem normal. Don't build habits that make certain sins seem worse than others. If you don't want to watch media that normalizes sexual sin, consider all varieties of this type of sin. On the other hand, if a show you are watching does have an LGBTQ+ character, this could be an opportunity for discussion and a good teaching moment for your family.

10. REMEMBER THE GOAL.

What *is* our goal when talking to others (including our LGBTQ+ kids) about these issues? Should we try to convince them not to avoid talking to their kids about LGBTQ+ issues if the children ask questions about those topics. You might (understandably!) want to avoid these questions out of fear of confusing your kids or telling them info they can't handle yet. And yes, you certainly don't need to overload your younger children with information they can't process. But there are age-appropriate ways to answer their questions without going into graphic detail. If you completely avoid talking about LGBTQ+ issues with your kids because you are afraid or uncomfortable, you will communicate that Christianity has no explanation for them, and your kids will go elsewhere to form their opinions.

9. EVALUATE YOUR MEDIA HABITS.

It's possible that you've made it a goal for your household to try not to consume

Our goal in listening should not be to win an argument or to change people. It should be to show people we love them, to learn about their experiences, and to empathize with them.

our resources to bless others and in the process realize they aren't much different from us. We invite them into our lives and are vulnerable with them. We become human to them, and they become human to us. If we treat others with respect and compassion, we make it much easier to discuss our contradictory points of view.

Mr. Bywater has practiced this principle in his own family. In high school, his oldest daughter became friends with a teenage boy who experienced gender dysphoria. Instead of being fearful or requiring her to cut off the friendship, the Bywaters invited the boy into their home and befriended him. Because they extended hospitality and respect to him, they were able to discuss sensitive topics like sexuality without offending one another.

6. WATCH YOUR LANGUAGE.

Avoid ostracizing language, even if you think the people around you won't be offended.[44] In multiple places, Scripture tells us that how we think in our hearts is even more important than how we behave outwardly.[45] In your home, do you talk about people in the LGBTQ+ community as though they were your enemy in some way? Do you use language like "the gays," "that's so gay" (i.e., stupid), or "the homosexual agenda"? If you do, your kids could learn to adopt this attitude from you. Or they will conclude that their LGBTQ+ friends are not welcome in your home. Such language also implies that you are somehow better than LGBTQ+ people, when in fact Christ loves us all equally.

Furthermore, there are many Christians who are same-sex attracted, but who recognize that acting on those desires is against what God commands and are doing their best to live celibate lives.[46] These people are courageous. Talking about all LGBTQ+ people derisively is not only hypocritical but also ignores those who wish they could act on those desires but are striving to honor Christ to the best of their ability.

7. TEACH YOUR KIDS BIBLICAL VIEWS OF MARRIAGE, SINGLENESS, MANHOOD, AND WOMANHOOD.

Promote biblical views on what it means to be a man or a woman, as well as on singleness and marriage. Marriage is a beautiful, noble, and holy calling. Singleness is also a beautiful, noble, and holy calling. Uphold both of them in your home. Educate yourself and your children about the biblical purpose of sexuality. Teach your kids what God says about what it means to be a man and what it means to be a woman so they understand the biblical alternative to what culture offers. Dr. Moore emphasizes the importance of supporting biblical statements about masculinity and femininity without supporting cultural stereotypes.[47] For example, if the church defines masculinity as loving sports or being aggressive, then men who are more verbal, empathetic, or artistic may feel they have no place in God's framework for sexuality. They could then be vulnerable to concluding that they must be gay, even though their strengths are completely valid within a heterosexual understanding of masculinity.

8. DON'T AVOID TALKING TO YOUR KIDS ABOUT LGBTQ+ ISSUES.

In his talk "Signposts: How Should You Talk to Your Children about Transgender Issues?"[48] Dr. Moore encourages parents

1. Why do gender and sexuality matter? What does the Bible say about the purpose of sexuality?

2. What do you think about what the Bible says about homosexuality?

3. Do you know anyone who has an LGBTQ+ identity? What do you know about their journey?

4. What do your friends think about LGBTQ+ issues? What shapes their opinions?

5. What is culture saying about the LGBTQ+ community in music, movies, and TV?

6. Do you think the internet has influenced what people believe about LGBTQ+ questions?

7. Do you think the church in general and our church in particular talk

about—and communicate with—the LGBTQ+ community in a helpful way?

8. Do you know anyone personally who is LGBTQ+ and who has been hurt by the church?

9. What could the church do to communicate the love (which includes the truth) of Christ to people in the LGBTQ+ community?

10. How would you feel if God asked you to stay single your whole life? Why?

11. What are some of the consequences when people believe they won't be happy unless they experience romantic love?

12. When Jesus tells His followers they will have to take up their crosses and follow Him,[49] do you think most people consider that doing so might

mean laying down their desires for romance, marriage, and having a family?

13. Have you ever been able to have a good conversation with someone with whom you strongly disagree? What is required to have such conversations?

CONCLUSION

EVERY GENERATION HAS ITS STRENGTHS and weaknesses. Gen Z is no different. One of the things it *has* gotten right is this: we need to love people as they are, no matter what. At the same time, many people embrace ideas that are opposed to God's commands—commands God gave us to help us flourish. Older generations tend to have a better understanding of how important it is not to compromise on the truth. Teenagers need the wisdom of older generations in their lives. If we are willing to listen to our kids and their friends, show that we value them, and treat them with respect, we will not only communicate the love Christ has for them, but we will also help them be open to what we have to say.

ADDITIONAL RESOURCES

NOTE: AXIS DOES NOT NECESSARILY AGREE *with all of the resources in this list.* **In fact, we totally disagree with some of them.** *However, there is value in considering all points of view before coming to a conclusion, if only to understand and empathize with other perspectives.*

1. The Center for Faith, Sexuality & Gender, https://www.centerforfaith.com/

2. Sexual & Gender Identity Institute, https://www.wheaton.edu/academics/school-of-psychology-counseling-and-family-therapy/sexual-and-gender-identity-institute/

3. "10 Things I Wish All Christian Leaders Knew about Gay Teens in Their Church," The Center for Faith, Sexuality & Gender, https://www.centerforfaith.com/blog/10-things-i-wish-all-christian-leaders-knew-about-gay-teens-in-their-church

4. Dr. Preston Sprinkle's Blog, https://www.prestonsprinkle.com/blog/

5. Authentic Intimacy, Dr. Juli Slattery, https://www.authenticintimacy.com/

6. *Q Ideas* Podcast (especially episodes 1–6)

7. Five Aspects Ministry, https://www.fiveaspects.com/

8. Posture Shift, https://postureshift.com/

9. iO Tillett Wright's TED Talk, https://www.youtube.com/watch?v=VAJ-5J21Rd0

10. The Council on Biblical Manhood and Womanhood, https://cbmw.org/

11. Dr. Russell Moore, https://www.russellmoore.com/category/topics/sexuality-and-gender/

12. "How Can the Church Help Those Battling Same-Sex Attraction?" The Gospel Coalition, https://www.thegospelcoalition.org/article/how-can-church-help-battle-same-sex-attraction/

13. "A Two-Minute Clip on Homosexuality Every Christian Should Watch," The Gospel Coalition, https://www.thegospelcoalition.org/article/two-minute-clip-homosexuality-every-christian-should-watch/

14. "What Christians Just Don't Get about LGBT Folks," The Gospel Coalition, https://www.thegospelcoalition.org /article/what-christians-just-dont-get -about-lgbt-folks/

15. Living Out (resource for Christians who experience same-sex attraction), https:// www.livingout.org/

16. "God, the Gospel, and the Gay Challenge—A Response to Matthew Vines," Dr. Albert Mohler, Jr., https:// albertmohler.com/2014/04/22/god -the-gospel-and-the-gay-challenge-a -response-to-matthew-vines

17. "Christianity and Homosexuality: A Review of Books," Dr. Timothy Keller, https://timothykeller.com/blog/2013 /10/4/christianity-and-homosexuality -a-review-of-books

18. "5 Questions with Caleb Kaltenbach, a Pastor Raised by Gay Parents," Boundless, https://www.boundless.org /blog/5-questions-with-caleb -kaltenbach-a-pastor-raised-by-gay -parents/

19. *Washed and Waiting: Reflections on Christian Faithfulness and Homosexuality* by Wesley Hill

20. *Out of a Far Country: A Gay Son's Journey to God. A Broken Mother's Search for Hope* by Christopher Yuan and Angela Yuan

21. *People to Be Loved: Why Homosexuality Is Not Just an Issue* by Preston Sprinkle

22. *Is God Anti-Gay?* (Questions Christians Ask) by Sam Allberry

23. *Same-Sex Marriage: A Thoughtful Approach to God's Design for Marriage* by Sean McDowell and John Stonestreet

24. *101 Frequently Asked Questions about Homosexuality* by Mike Haley

25. *God and the Gay Christian: The Biblical Case in Support of Same-Sex Relationships* by Matthew Vines

26. *The Inner Voice of Love: A Journey through Anguish to Freedom* by Henri Nouwen

NOTES

1. Molly Driscoll, "Ellen DeGeneres Popularity Demonstrated with a Record Number of People's Choice Awards," *Christian Science Monitor*, January 19, 2017, https://www. csmonitor.com/The-Culture/TV/2017/0119 /Ellen-DeGeneres-popularity-demonstrated -with-a-record-number-of-People-s-Choice -Awards.

2. Valentina Zarya, "President Obama Gets 'Choked Up' while Giving Ellen DeGeneres the Highest Civilian Honor," *Fortune*, November 23, 2016, https://fortune.com/2016/11/23 /obama-ellen-degeneres-medal/.

3. Hanna Flanagan, "Harry Styles Models a Gucci Gown as He Becomes the First Man to Land a Solo Cover of *Vogue*," *People*, November 13, 2020, https://people.com/style/harry-styles -wears-a-dress-on-the-cover-of-vogue/.

4. "What Is LGBTQQIAAP?," Decahedron of Q, accessed May 31, 2022, https://decahedron ofq.wordpress.com/what-is-lgbtqqiaap/.

5. Lauren Chen, "Two Genders. Two.," YouTube, video, 8:32, April 17, 2017, https://www.youtube.com/watch?v=69QBODgzJI8.

6. Cydney Adams, "The Difference between Sexual Orientation and Gender Identity," CBS News, March 24, 2017, https://www.cbsnews.com/news/the-difference-between-sexual-orientation-and-gender-identity/.

7. Sam Killermann, "Comprehensive* List of LGBTQ+ Vocabulary Definitions," It's Pronounced Metrosexual, accessed May 31, 2022, https://www.itspronouncedmetrosexual.com/2013/01/a-comprehensive-list-of-lgbtq-term-definitions/.

8. "LGBTQI+ Glossary of Terms," We Are Family, accessed May 31, 2022, https://wearefamilycharleston.org/lgbt-glossary-az.

9. "Glossary of Terms: LGBTQ," GLAAD Media Reference Guide, 11th edition, accessed May 31, 2022, https://www.glaad.org/reference/terms.

10. Kate Shellnutt, "Get Ready, Youth Group Leaders: Teens Twice as Likely to Identify as Atheist or LGBT," *Christianity Today*, January

23, 2018, https://www.christianitytoday.com
/news/2018/january/youth-group-leaders
-generation-z-atheist-lgbt-teens-barna.html.

11. Rachel Hosie, "Two Thirds of 16 to 22-Year-
Olds Say They Are Only Attracted to the
Opposite Sex," *Independent*, September 27,
2017, https://www.independent.co.uk/life
-style/opposite-sex-only-attracted-young
-people-16-to-22-heterosexual-bi-lgbt
-a7969876.html.

12. Emily A. Greytak et al., *From Teasing to
Torment: School Climate Revisited, A Survey
of U.S. Secondary School Students and
Teachers* (New York: GLSEN, 2016), https://
www.glsen.org/research/teasing-torment
-school-climate-revisited-survey-us-seconda.

13. Juli Slattery, "#200: Listening So People Will
Talk," Authentic Intimacy, March 26, 2018,
https://www.authenticintimacy.com/resources
/8029/200-listening-so-people-will-talk.

14. Megan McIntyre, "What the World Needs Now
Is More Ruby Rose," Refinery29, June 4, 2016,
https://www.refinery29.com/en-us/ruby-rose
-urban-decay-vice-lipstick-interview.

15. "World of Belonging," Disney, accessed May 31, 2022, https://impact.disney.com/diversity -inclusion/.

16. André Wheeler, "Lil Nas X: 'I 100% Want to Represent the LGBT Community,'" *Guardian*, April 4, 2020, https://www.theguardian.com /music/2020/apr/04/lil-nas-x-i-100-want-to -represent-the-lgbt-community.

17. Noah Michelson, "Lady Gaga Had Something to Say about LGBTQ Equality on Opening Night of Her 'Joanne' Tour," *HuffPost*, August 2, 2017, https://www.huffpost.com/entry/lady -gaga-joanne-tour-lgbtq_n_598227dae4b0 fa1575fbc0b5.

18. Jake Hall, "Is Miley Cyrus the Best Spokesperson for LGBT Issues?" Highsnobiety, accessed May 31, 2022, https://www .highsnobiety.com/p/miley-cyrus-lgbt/.

19. Suzannah Weiss, "Halsey Debunks Myth about Bisexuality on Twitter," *Teen Vogue*, December 19, 2017, https://www.teenvogue .com/story/halsey-debunks-myth-about -bisexuality-on-twitter.

20. Hayley Kiyoko, "Girls Like Girls," YouTube, video, 4:59, June 24, 2015, https://www.youtube.com/watch?v=I0MT8SwNa_U.

21. Steven J. Horowitz, "Hayley Kiyoko on Her Debut Album 'Expectations' and Being a Queer Pop Star: 'It's Important for People to Lead by Example,'" *Billboard*, March 8, 2018, https://www.billboard.com/music/pop/hayley-kiyoko-interview-expectations-sexuality-8235955/.

22. Nick Duffy, "Taylor Swift Addresses Homophobia in the Music Industry after Hayley Kiyoko Comments," Pink News, April 1, 2018, https://www.pinknews.co.uk/2018/04/01/taylor-swift-addresses-homophobia-in-the-music-industry-after-hayley-kiyoko-comments/.

23. Taylor Swift, "You Need to Calm Down," YouTube, video, 3:30, June 17, 2019, https://www.youtube.com/watch?v=Dkk9gvTmCXY.

24. iO Tillett Wright, "Self Evident Truths: 10,000 Portraits of Queer America," 2010–2020, http://www.selfevidentproject.com/about.

25. Olivia Blair, "Lily-Rose Depp Clarifies Comments on Her Sexuality," *Independent*, February 4, 2016, https://www.independent.co.uk/news /people/lilyrose-depp-clarifies-comments -about-her-sexuality-a6853151.html.

26. Connor Franta, "Coming Out," YouTube, video, 6:27, December 8, 2014, https://www.youtube .com/watch?v=WYodBfRxKWI&t=315s.

27. Milo Stewart, YouTube, https://www.youtube .com/user/RoryDeganRepresent.

28. NikkieTutorials, "I'm Coming Out.," YouTube, video, 17:13, January 13, 2020, https://www .youtube.com/watch?v=QOOw2E_qAsE.

29. Leslie Walker, "How to Edit Your Gender Identity on Facebook," Lifewire, updated October 20, 2021, https://www.lifewire.com/edit-gender -identity-status-on-facebook-2654421.

30. Bené Viera, "10 Young Celebs Who Talk Openly about Their Sexuality," *Teen Vogue*, February 11, 2016, https://www.teenvogue .com/gallery/10-celebs-openly-discuss-their -sexuality#3.

31. XXXTENTACION, "XXXTENTACION - SAD!," YouTube, video, 2:46, March 1, 2018, https://www.youtube.com/watch?v=pgN-vvVVxMA.

32. Q Ideas, "Episode 002 The Gay Conversation | Theology: Not What the Bible Says, but What It Means," *Q Ideas* podcast, January 21, 2016, https://qpodcast.libsyn.com/page/10/size/25.

33. BBC Three, "Things Not to Say to a Non-Binary Person," YouTube, video, 6:51, June 27, 2017, https://www.youtube.com/watch?v=8b4MZjMVgdk.

34. Jonathan Merritt, "The Politics of Jen Hatmaker: Trump, Black Lives Matter, Gay Marriage and More," Religion News Service, October 25, 2016, https://religionnews.com/2016/10/25/the-politics-of-jen-hatmaker-trump-black-lives-matter-gay-marriage-and-more/.

35. Jay Dee, "When Did God Stop Allowing Multiple Wives," Uncovering Intimacy, May 16, 2015, https://www.uncoveringintimacy.com/when-did-god-stop-allowing-multiple-wives/.

36. See Matthew 19:4.

37. Juli Slattery, *Rethinking Sexuality: God's Design and Why It Matters* (Colorado Springs, CO: Multnomah, 2018), 53.

38. Preston Sprinkle, "Put Homophobia to Death," Theology in the Raw, December 10, 2015, https://theologyintheraw.kinsta.cloud/blog /2015/12/put-homophobia-to-death/.

39. The Center for Faith, "Dear Church: I'm Gay," Vimeo, video, 20:38, https://vimeo.com /231166638.

40. "#200: Listening So People Will Talk," podcast, Authentic Intimacy, March 26, 2018, https:// www.authenticintimacy.com/resources ?CoBrandedOnly=znkycbnbrsnt&page=24.

41. Megan Phelps-Roper, "I Grew Up in the Westboro Baptist Church. Here's Why I Left," TED Talk, YouTube, video, 15:17, March 6, 2017, https://www.youtube.com/watch?v =bVV2Zk88beY.

42. See Romans 3:23.

43. Kevin James Bywater, "Hospitality, Not Tolerance," KJB: Kevin James Bywater, accessed May 31, 2022, https://www.kevinbywater.com /blog.

44. Preston Sprinkle, "How to Talk about Homosexuality: 6 Things Every Straight Christian Should Know," Theology in the Raw, May 7, 2015, https://theologyintheraw.kinsta. cloud/blog/2015/05/how-to-talk-about -homosexuality-6-things-every-straight -christian-should-know/.

45. See Matthew 23:27-28.

46. Preston Sprinkle, "Growing Up Gay and Christian," Theology in the Raw, January 19, 2016, https://theologyintheraw.kinsta.cloud /blog/2016/01/growing-up-gay-and-christian/.

47. Russell Moore, "Topic: Sexuality and Gender," RussellMoore.com, accessed May 31, 2022, https://www.russellmoore.com/category /topics/sexuality-and-gender/.

48. Moore, "Topic: Sexuality and Gender."

49. See Matthew 16:24-26.

PARENT GUIDES TO SOCIAL MEDIA
BY AXIS

It's common to feel lost in your teen's world. Let these be your go-to guides on social media, how it affects your teen, and how to begin an ongoing conversation about faith that matters.

BUNDLE THESE 5 BOOKS AND SAVE